18 Month
CALENDAR FOR WRITERS

June 2021 through Dec 2022

INDEPENDENTLY PUBLISHED

"We will open the book. Its pages are blank. We are going to put words on them ourselves. The book is called Opportunity and its first chapter is New Year's Day."
~ Edith Lovejoy Pierce

"There is nothing like a new calendar with its expectant little blocks of dates waiting to be filled in with the year's days and nights of living and writing."
~ Kimberly Coleman

INDEPENDENTLY PUBLISHED

ISBN 978 0 578 82372 0

Photo Credits:
Front Cover: © Olena 1983 www.fotosearch.ie
Title Page: Silhouette Firebird © Derriva www.fotosearch.ie
'2021', '2022', '2023', '2024' © DmitryGuzhanin www.fotosearch.ie
'writer' © franckito www.fotosearch.ie
'a valentine' © frescomovie www.fotosearch.ie
'chameleon' © puhimec www.fotosearch.ie
'slate Phoenix' © Olena 1983 www.fotosearch.ie
'tribute' © nak1 www.fotosearch.ie
'black raven' © Creative_Hearts www.fotosearch.ie
'The Kestrel' © Richard Winters

Other Photos and Illustrations courtesy of Pixabay

_____

Cover and Interior Design by Kimberly Coleman,
Creator of the Bestselling **Calendar For Writers** *Series*

INDEPENDENTLY PUBLISHED

It was almost mid-year when my husband and I moved to Ireland so on our early shopping trips I would search for a new 18 Month Calendar. There were no 18 Month Calendars apparently anywhere on this island.

In the States I always bought a new calendar just before Summer…I was always out of love with the one I'd scribbled in since Christmas (and truthfully, by May there were more than a few coffee stains…….). There was never any room to write anything more by then, I'd filled up the margins with story ideas and plans, I would even resort to writing across the full-page photos! I stuffed loose leaf papers in my purchased calendars, but it just wasn't working to help my ADD get on track to write and get something *finished*. That's when I designed my ideal Calendar/Workbook (in 2016) and began publishing these for other writers on the chance they'd find them useful too.

Since then, I have printed new ones every year for my own use; if other people find them beneficial, all the better. These essential workbooks keep me on track with my writing by forcing my ADD to focus on those 29 or 30 little boxes of 'things to do'…. at least for a little while. Note pages are meant to capture those fleeting ideas, the early morning ones before coffee and sometimes the extremely late night ones that I can't remember a minute more if I didn't write them down! … I keep a pen attached to the front cover of my Calendar (once again this rescues my ADD from an hour's hunt for a functioning ink pen….). This too increases the amount of writing I do. *Memory grows more fleeting once the laundry stacks up at our house.* I *have* to make notes if I am to remember anything by sunset!

Since I have become more organized these past years, I've written three Amazon Bestsellers (two are under my pen name). Using a calendar, planning ahead, writing out my goals, my thoughts, competitions I might enter, just using the calendar to communicate with myself…this has helped me enormously as a writer. I've noticed a marked increase in my daily productivity. I check my Calendar daily and almost always add in something, somewhere, on it. All my current, important papers and notes are stashed in it (again, why the size and binding are important to me).

I hope you will find my *Calendar For Writers* useful in writing your Bestseller! …and I hope you will let me know. It is fantastic hearing how my simple books have helped so many of you over the years!

Kimberly Coleman
Designer and Creator of the
Bestselling *Calendar For Writers* Series

———————————

A Very Special Section…

with extra monthly calendars plus several Note Pages for the first six months of the New Year!

Additional writing pages are also appended and as usual, follow each month from June 2021 through December 2022.

Start NOW on the next two years of your writing plans!!

———

It was almost mid-year when my husband and I moved to Ireland so on our early shopping trips I would search for a new 18 Month Calendar. There were no 18 Month Calendars apparently anywhere on this island.

In the States I always bought a new calendar just before Summer…I was always out of love with the one I'd scribbled in since Christmas (and truthfully, by May there were more than a few coffee stains…….). There was never any room to write anything more by then, I'd filled up the margins with story ideas and plans, I would even resort to writing across the full-page photos! I stuffed loose leaf papers in my purchased calendars, but it just wasn't working to help my ADD get on track to write and get something *finished*. That's when I designed my ideal Calendar/Workbook (in 2016) and began publishing these for other writers on the chance they'd find them useful too.

Since then, I have printed new ones every year for my own use; if other people find them beneficial, all the better. These essential workbooks keep me on track with my writing by forcing my ADD to focus on those 29 or 30 little boxes of 'things to do'…. at least for a little while. Note pages are meant to capture those fleeting ideas, the early morning ones before coffee and sometimes the extremely late night ones that I can't remember a minute more if I didn't write them down! … I keep a pen attached to the front cover of my Calendar (once again this rescues my ADD from an hour's hunt for a functioning ink pen….). This too increases the amount of writing I do. *Memory grows more fleeting once the laundry stacks up at our house.* I *have* to make notes if I am to remember anything by sunset!

Since I have become more organized these past years, I've written three Amazon Bestsellers (two are under my pen name). Using a calendar, planning ahead, writing out my goals, my thoughts, competitions I might enter, just using the calendar to communicate with myself…this has helped me enormously as a writer. I've noticed a marked increase in my daily productivity. I check my Calendar daily and almost always add in something, somewhere, on it. All my current, important papers and notes are stashed in it (again, why the size and binding are important to me).

I hope you will find my *Calendar For Writers* useful in writing your Bestseller! …and I hope you will let me know. It is fantastic hearing how my simple books have helped so many of you over the years!

Kimberly Coleman
Designer and Creator of the
Bestselling *Calendar For Writers* Series

————————————

A Very Special
Section...

*with extra monthly
calendars plus several
Note Pages for the
first six months of the
New Year!*

*Additional writing
pages are also
appended and as
usual, follow each
month from June 2021
through December
2022.*

*Start NOW on the
next two years of
your writing plans!!*

———

2021

January

Su	Mo	Tu	We	Th	Fr	Sa
					1	2
3	4	5	6	7	8	9
10	11	12	13	14	15	16
17	18	19	20	21	22	23
24	25	26	27	28	29	30
31						

February

Su	Mo	Tu	We	Th	Fr	Sa
	1	2	3	4	5	6
7	8	9	10	11	12	13
14	15	16	17	18	19	20
21	22	23	24	25	26	27
28						

March

Su	Mo	Tu	We	Th	Fr	Sa
	1	2	3	4	5	6
7	8	9	10	11	12	13
14	15	16	17	18	19	20
21	22	23	24	25	26	27
28	29	30	31			

April

Su	Mo	Tu	We	Th	Fr	Sa
				1	2	3
4	5	6	7	8	9	10
11	12	13	14	15	16	17
18	19	20	21	22	23	24
25	26	27	28	29	30	

May

Su	Mo	Tu	We	Th	Fr	Sa
						1
2	3	4	5	6	7	8
9	10	11	12	13	14	15
16	17	18	19	20	21	22
23	24	25	26	27	28	29
30	31					

June

Su	Mo	Tu	We	Th	Fr	Sa
		1	2	3	4	5
6	7	8	9	10	11	12
13	14	15	16	17	18	19
20	21	22	23	24	25	26
27	28	29	30			

July

Su	Mo	Tu	We	Th	Fr	Sa
				1	2	3
4	5	6	7	8	9	10
11	12	13	14	15	16	17
18	19	20	21	22	23	24
25	26	27	28	29	30	31

August

Su	Mo	Tu	We	Th	Fr	Sa
1	2	3	4	5	6	7
8	9	10	11	12	13	14
15	16	17	18	19	20	21
22	23	24	25	26	27	28
29	30	31				

September

Su	Mo	Tu	We	Th	Fr	Sa
			1	2	3	4
5	6	7	8	9	10	11
12	13	14	15	16	17	18
19	20	21	22	23	24	25
26	27	28	29	30		

October

Su	Mo	Tu	We	Th	Fr	Sa
					1	2
3	4	5	6	7	8	9
10	11	12	13	14	15	16
17	18	19	20	21	22	23
24	25	26	27	28	29	30
31						

November

Su	Mo	Tu	We	Th	Fr	Sa
	1	2	3	4	5	6
7	8	9	10	11	12	13
14	15	16	17	18	19	20
21	22	23	24	25	26	27
28	29	30				

December

Su	Mo	Tu	We	Th	Fr	Sa
			1	2	3	4
5	6	7	8	9	10	11
12	13	14	15	16	17	18
19	20	21	22	23	24	25
26	27	28	29	30	31	

JANUARY 2021

Sun	Mon	Tue	Wed	Thu	Fri	Sat
					1 New Year's Day	2
3	4	5	6	7	8	9
10	11	12	13	14	15	16
17	18 Martin Luther King Jr. Holiday	19	20 Inauguration Day	21	22	23
24	25	26	27	28 Data Protection Day (Ireland and UK)	29	30
31	**NOTES**					

"Close the door. Write with no one looking over your shoulder.
Don't try to figure out what other people want to hear from you;
figure out what you have to say. It's the one and only thing you have to offer."
~ Barbara Kingsolver

FEBRUARY 2021

Sun	Mon	Tue	Wed	Thu	Fri	Sat
	1	2 Groundhog Day	3	4	5	6
7	8	9	10	11	12	13
14 Valentine's Day	15 Presidents Day	16	17 Ash Wednesday	18	19	20
21	22	23	24	25	26	27
28	**NOTES**					

*"So long as you write what you wish to write,
that is all that matters; and whether it matters for ages
or only for hours, nobody can say."*
— *Virginia Woolf*

MARCH 2021

Sun	Mon	Tue	Wed	Thu	Fri	Sat
	1	2	3	4	5	6
7	8	9	10	11	12	13
14 Daylight Saving Begins	15	16	17 St. Patrick's Day	18	19	20 First Day of Spring
21	22	23	24	25	26	27
28	29	30	31	**NOTES**		

*"Above all things -- read. Read the great stylists who cannot
be copied rather than the successful writers who must not be copied."*
— *Ngaio Marsh*

_____

_____

_____

_____

_____

_____

_____

_____

_____

APRIL 2021

Sun	Mon	Tue	Wed	Thu	Fri	Sat
				1	2 Good Friday	3
4 Easter	5 Easter Monday	6	7	8	9	10
11	12	13	14	15	16	17
18	19	20	21	22 Earth Day	23	24
25	26	27	28	29	30 Arbor Day	

"What matters most is how well you walk through the fire."
— Charles Bukowski

MAY 2021

Sun	Mon	Tue	Wed	Thu	Fri	Sat
						1
2	3 May Day	4	5 Cinco De Mayo	6	7	8
9	10	11	12	13	14	15
16	17	18	19	20	21	22
23	24	25	26	27	28	29
30	31 Memorial Day Bank Holiday (UK)	**NOTES**				

"My first feeling was that there was no way to continue. Writing isn't like math; in math, two plus two always equals four no matter what your mood is like. With writing, the way you feel changes everything."
~ Stephenie Meyer

- - - - - - - - -

JUNE 2021

Sun	Mon	Tue	Wed	Thu	Fri	Sat
		1	2	3	4	5
6	7 Bank Holiday (Ireland)	8	9	10	11	12
13	14 Flag Day	15	16	17	18	19
20 First Day of Summer	21	22	23	24	25	26
27	28	29	30	**NOTES**		

*"Some battles are won with swords and spears,
others with quills and ravens."*
~ George R. R. Martin

———

JULY 2021

Sun	Mon	Tue	Wed	Thu	Fri	Sat
				1	2	3
4 Independence Day	5	6	7	8	9	10
11	12 Battle of the Boyne	13	14	15	16	17
18	19	20	21	22	23	24
25	26	27	28	29	30	31

AUGUST 2021

Sun	Mon	Tue	Wed	Thu	Fri	Sat
1	2 Bank Holiday (Ireland)	3	4	5	6	7
8	9	10	11	12	13	14
15	16	17	18	19	20	21
22	23	24	25	26	27	28
29	30 Bank Holiday (UK)	31	**NOTES**			

SEPTEMBER 2021

Sun	Mon	Tue	Wed	Thu	Fri	Sat
			1	2	3	4
5	6 Labor Day	7	8	9	10	11
12	13	14	15	16	17	18
19	20	21	22 First Day of Autumn	23	24	25
26	27	28	29	30	NOTES	

OCTOBER 2021

Sun	Mon	Tue	Wed	Thu	Fri	Sat
					1	2
3	4	5	6	7	8	9
10	11 Columbus Day	12	13	14	15	16
17	18	19	20	21	22	23
24	25 Bank Holiday (Ireland and UK)	26	27	28	29	30
31 Halloween	NOTES					

Crazy how time flies!

November is quickly approaching...
Throughout our years on Twitter, we've seen thousands of people challenge themselves to write a novel that particular month as part of a virtual team structure.

If you will be participating, we have just the book for that!
Our glossy, paperback **30 Day Writing Notebook** is sold worldwide (ask for it by title from your local bookshop; published by IngramSpark). Be aware it is large format, over 250 pages, 8x10in (a4), with narrow lines – enough to write your novel in a month. Check out additional details and interior snips on our Twitter stream (@heath_and_bog and @kurtseapoint).

_____

_____

_____

_____

_____

_____

_____

_____

_____

_____

_____

_____

_____

November 2021

Sun	Mon	Tue	Wed	Thu	Fri	Sat
	1	2 Election Day	3	4	5	6
7 Daylight Saving Time Ends	8	9	10	11 Veterans Day	12	13
14	15	16	17	18	19	20
21	22	23	24	25 Thanksgiving Day	26 Black Friday	27
28	29 Cyber Monday	30	**NOTES**			

"To acquire the habit of reading is to construct for yourself
a refuge from almost all the miseries of life."
— W. Somerset Maugham

*winter*_____

DECEMBER 2021

Sun	Mon	Tue	Wed	Thu	Fri	Sat
			1	2	3	4
5	6	7	8	9	10	11
12	13	14	15	16	17	18
19	20	21 First Day of Winter	22	23	24	25 Christmas
26 St. Stephen's Day (Ireland) Boxing Day (UK)	27	28	29	30	31	

2021 in Review

"The years go by. The time, it does fly. Every single second is
a moment in time that passes. And it seems like nothing –
but when you're looking back ... well, it amounts to everything."
— Ray Bradbury

_____

_____

_____

_____

_____

_____

_____

_____

_____

_____

_____

_____

_____

_____

_____

_____

2022 Initial Plans

"The trouble with 'if only' is that it doesn't change anything.
It keeps the person facing the wrong way – backward instead of forward.
It wastes time. In the end, if you let it become a habit,
it can become a real roadblock – an excuse for not trying anymore."
— Arthur Gordon

_____

_____

_____

_____

_____

_____

_____

_____

_____

_____

_____

_____

_____

_____

_____

_____

2022

January

Su	Mo	Tu	We	Th	Fr	Sa
						1
2	3	4	5	6	7	8
9	10	11	12	13	14	15
16	17	18	19	20	21	22
23	24	25	26	27	28	29
30	31					

February

Su	Mo	Tu	We	Th	Fr	Sa
		1	2	3	4	5
6	7	8	9	10	11	12
13	14	15	16	17	18	19
20	21	22	23	24	25	26
27	28					

March

Su	Mo	Tu	We	Th	Fr	Sa
		1	2	3	4	5
6	7	8	9	10	11	12
13	14	15	16	17	18	19
20	21	22	23	24	25	26
27	28	29	30	31		

April

Su	Mo	Tu	We	Th	Fr	Sa
					1	2
3	4	5	6	7	8	9
10	11	12	13	14	15	16
17	18	19	20	21	22	23
24	25	26	27	28	29	30

May

Su	Mo	Tu	We	Th	Fr	Sa
1	2	3	4	5	6	7
8	9	10	11	12	13	14
15	16	17	18	19	20	21
22	23	24	25	26	27	28
29	30	31				

June

Su	Mo	Tu	We	Th	Fr	Sa
			1	2	3	4
5	6	7	8	9	10	11
12	13	14	15	16	17	18
19	20	21	22	23	24	25
26	27	28	29	30		

July

Su	Mo	Tu	We	Th	Fr	Sa
					1	2
3	4	5	6	7	8	9
10	11	12	13	14	15	16
17	18	19	20	21	22	23
24	25	26	27	28	29	30
31						

August

Su	Mo	Tu	We	Th	Fr	Sa
	1	2	3	4	5	6
7	8	9	10	11	12	13
14	15	16	17	18	19	20
21	22	23	24	25	26	27
28	29	30	31			

September

Su	Mo	Tu	We	Th	Fr	Sa
				1	2	3
4	5	6	7	8	9	10
11	12	13	14	15	16	17
18	19	20	21	22	23	24
25	26	27	28	29	30	

October

Su	Mo	Tu	We	Th	Fr	Sa
						1
2	3	4	5	6	7	8
9	10	11	12	13	14	15
16	17	18	19	20	21	22
23	24	25	26	27	28	29
30	31					

November

Su	Mo	Tu	We	Th	Fr	Sa
		1	2	3	4	5
6	7	8	9	10	11	12
13	14	15	16	17	18	19
20	21	22	23	24	25	26
27	28	29	30			

December

Su	Mo	Tu	We	Th	Fr	Sa
				1	2	3
4	5	6	7	8	9	10
11	12	13	14	15	16	17
18	19	20	21	22	23	24
25	26	27	28	29	30	31

Books to Read

Etc

_____

_____

_____

_____

_____

_____

_____

_____

_____

_____

_____

_____

_____

_____

_____

_____

_____

_____

_____

_____

_____

JANUARY 2022

Sun	Mon	Tue	Wed	Thu	Fri	Sat
						1 New Year's Day
2	3	4	5	6	7	8
9	10	11	12	13	14	15
16	17 Martin Luther King Jr Holiday.	18	19	20	21	22
23	24	25	26	27	28 Data Protection Day (Ireland and UK)	29
30	31	NOTES				

FEBRUARY 2022

Sun	Mon	Tue	Wed	Thu	Fri	Sat
		1	2 Groundhog Day	3	4	5
6	7	8	9	10	11	12
13	14 Valentine's Day	15	16	17	18	19
20	21 Presidents Day	22	23	24	25	26
27	28	**NOTES**				

"In books I have traveled, not only to other worlds, but into my own."
— Anna Quindlen

———————————————

"We read books to find out who we are.
What other people, real or imaginary,
do and think and feel... is an essential
guide to our understanding of what
we ourselves are and may become."
— Ursula K. LeGuin

spring

MARCH 2022

Sun	Mon	Tue	Wed	Thu	Fri	Sat
		1	2	3	4	5
6	7	8	9	10	11	12
13 Daylight Saving Begins	14	15	16	17 St. Patrick's Day	18	19
20 First Day of Spring	21	22	23	24	25	26
27	28	29	30	31	NOTES	

APRIL 2022

Sun	Mon	Tue	Wed	Thu	Fri	Sat
					1	2
3	4	5	6	7	8	9
10	11	12	13	14	15 Good Friday	16
17 Easter	18 Easter Monday	19	20	21	22 Earth Day	23
24	25	26	27	28	29 Arbor Day	30

MAY 2022

Sun	Mon	Tue	Wed	Thu	Fri	Sat
1	2 May Day	3	4	5 Cinco De Mayo	6	7
8	9	10	11	12	13	14
15	16	17	18	19	20	21
22	23	24	25	26	27	28
29	30 Memorial Day Bank Holiday (UK)	31	**NOTES**			

"Man reading should be man intensely alive.
The book should be a ball of light in one's hand."
— Ezra Pound

———

"To learn to read is to light a fire;
every syllable that is spelled out is a spark."
— Victor Hugo

———

"One glance at a book and you hear the voice
of another person, perhaps someone dead
for 1,000 years. To read is to voyage through time."
— Carl Sagan

summer_____

JUNE 2022

Sun	Mon	Tue	Wed	Thu	Fri	Sat
			1	2	3	4
5	6 Bank Holiday (Ireland)	7	8	9	10	11
12	13	14 Flag Day	15	16	17	18
19	20	21 First Day of Summer	22	23	24	25
26	27	28	29	30	NOTES	

JULY 2022

Sun	Mon	Tue	Wed	Thu	Fri	Sat
					1	2
3	4 Independence Day	5	6	7 Battle of the Boyne (UK)	8	9
10	11	12	13	14	15	16
17	18	19	20	21	22	23
24	25	26	27	28	29	30
31	**NOTES**					

AUGUST 2022

Sun	Mon	Tue	Wed	Thu	Fri	Sat
	1 Bank Holiday (Ireland)	2	3	4	5	6
7	8	9	10	11	12	13
14	15	16	17	18	19	20
21	22	23	24	25	26	27
28	29 Bank Holiday (UK)	30	31	NOTES		

"I'm so glad I live in a world where there are Octobers."
— L M Montgomery

———————————

"Aprils have never meant much to me,
autumns seem that season of beginning, spring."
— Truman Capote

———————————

"Once in a while I am struck all over again... by just how blue
the sky appears ...on wind-played autumn mornings, blue enough
to bruise a heart."
— Sanober Khan

*autumn*_____

SEPTEMBER 2022

Sun	Mon	Tue	Wed	Thu	Fri	Sat
			1	2	3
4	5 Labor Day	6	7	8	9	10
11	12	13	14	15	16	17
18	19	20	21	22	23 First Day of Autumn	24
25	26	27	28	29	30	NOTES

OCTOBER 2022

Sun	Mon	Tue	Wed	Thu	Fri	Sat
						1
2	3	4	5	6	7	8
9	10 Columbus Day	11	12	13	14	15
16	17	18	19	20	21	22
23	24	25	26	27	28	29
30	31 Halloween	NOTES				

NOVEMBER 2022

Sun	Mon	Tue	Wed	Thu	Fri	Sat
		1	2	3	4	5
6 Daylight Saving Time Ends	7	8 Election Day	9	10	11 Veterans Day	12
13	14	15	16	17	18	19
20	21	22	23	24 Thanksgiving Day	25 Black Friday	26
27	28 Cyber Monday	29	30	**NOTES**		

winter

"In the winter she curls up around a good book and dreams away the cold."
— Ben Aaronovitch

DECEMBER 2022

Sun	Mon	Tue	Wed	Thu	Fri	Sat
				1	2	3
4	5	6	7	8	9	10
11	12	13	14	15	16	17
18	19	20	21 First Day of Winter	22	23	24
25 Christmas	26 St. Stephen's Day (Ireland) Boxing Day (UK)	27	28	29	30	31

2023

January

Su	Mo	Tu	We	Th	Fr	Sa
1	2	3	4	5	6	7
8	9	10	11	12	13	14
15	16	17	18	19	20	21
22	23	24	25	26	27	28
29	30	31				

February

Su	Mo	Tu	We	Th	Fr	Sa
			1	2	3	4
5	6	7	8	9	10	11
12	13	14	15	16	17	18
19	20	21	22	23	24	25
26	27	28				

March

Su	Mo	Tu	We	Th	Fr	Sa
			1	2	3	4
5	6	7	8	9	10	11
12	13	14	15	16	17	18
19	20	21	22	23	24	25
26	27	28	29	30	31	

April

Su	Mo	Tu	We	Th	Fr	Sa
						1
2	3	4	5	6	7	8
9	10	11	12	13	14	15
16	17	18	19	20	21	22
23	24	25	26	27	28	29
30						

May

Su	Mo	Tu	We	Th	Fr	Sa
	1	2	3	4	5	6
7	8	9	10	11	12	13
14	15	16	17	18	19	20
21	22	23	24	25	26	27
28	29	30	31			

June

Su	Mo	Tu	We	Th	Fr	Sa
				1	2	3
4	5	6	7	8	9	10
11	12	13	14	15	16	17
18	19	20	21	22	23	24
25	26	27	28	29	30	

July

Su	Mo	Tu	We	Th	Fr	Sa
						1
2	3	4	5	6	7	8
9	10	11	12	13	14	15
16	17	18	19	20	21	22
23	24	25	26	27	28	29
30	31					

August

Su	Mo	Tu	We	Th	Fr	Sa
		1	2	3	4	5
6	7	8	9	10	11	12
13	14	15	16	17	18	19
20	21	22	23	24	25	26
27	28	29	30	31		

September

Su	Mo	Tu	We	Th	Fr	Sa
					1	2
3	4	5	6	7	8	9
10	11	12	13	14	15	16
17	18	19	20	21	22	23
24	25	26	27	28	29	30

October

Su	Mo	Tu	We	Th	Fr	Sa
1	2	3	4	5	6	7
8	9	10	11	12	13	14
15	16	17	18	19	20	21
22	23	24	25	26	27	28
29	30	31				

November

Su	Mo	Tu	We	Th	Fr	Sa
			1	2	3	4
5	6	7	8	9	10	11
12	13	14	15	16	17	18
19	20	21	22	23	24	25
26	27	28	29	30		

December

Su	Mo	Tu	We	Th	Fr	Sa
					1	2
3	4	5	6	7	8	9
10	11	12	13	14	15	16
17	18	19	20	21	22	23
24	25	26	27	28	29	30
31						

"The reason birds can fly, and we can't is simply because they have perfect faith, for to have faith is to have wings."
— J.M. Barrie

The Kestrel *by Richard Winters*

2024

January
Su	Mo	Tu	We	Th	Fr	Sa
	1	2	3	4	5	6
7	8	9	10	11	12	13
14	15	16	17	18	19	20
21	22	23	24	25	26	27
28	29	30	31			

February
Su	Mo	Tu	We	Th	Fr	Sa
				1	2	3
4	5	6	7	8	9	10
11	12	13	14	15	16	17
18	19	20	21	22	23	24
25	26	27	28	29		

March
Su	Mo	Tu	We	Th	Fr	Sa
					1	2
3	4	5	6	7	8	9
10	11	12	13	14	15	16
17	18	19	20	21	22	23
24	25	26	27	28	29	30
31						

April
Su	Mo	Tu	We	Th	Fr	Sa
	1	2	3	4	5	6
7	8	9	10	11	12	13
14	15	16	17	18	19	20
21	22	23	24	25	26	27
28	29	30				

May
Su	Mo	Tu	We	Th	Fr	Sa
			1	2	3	4
5	6	7	8	9	10	11
12	13	14	15	16	17	18
19	20	21	22	23	24	25
26	27	28	29	30	31	

June
Su	Mo	Tu	We	Th	Fr	Sa
						1
2	3	4	5	6	7	8
9	10	11	12	13	14	15
16	17	18	19	20	21	22
23	24	25	26	27	28	29
30						

July
Su	Mo	Tu	We	Th	Fr	Sa
	1	2	3	4	5	6
7	8	9	10	11	12	13
14	15	16	17	18	19	20
21	22	23	24	25	26	27
28	29	30	31			

August
Su	Mo	Tu	We	Th	Fr	Sa
				1	2	3
4	5	6	7	8	9	10
11	12	13	14	15	16	17
18	19	20	21	22	23	24
25	26	27	28	29	30	31

September
Su	Mo	Tu	We	Th	Fr	Sa
1	2	3	4	5	6	7
8	9	10	11	12	13	14
15	16	17	18	19	20	21
22	23	24	25	26	27	28
29	30					

October
Su	Mo	Tu	We	Th	Fr	Sa
		1	2	3	4	5
6	7	8	9	10	11	12
13	14	15	16	17	18	19
20	21	22	23	24	25	26
27	28	29	30	31		

November
Su	Mo	Tu	We	Th	Fr	Sa
					1	2
3	4	5	6	7	8	9
10	11	12	13	14	15	16
17	18	19	20	21	22	23
24	25	26	27	28	29	30

December
Su	Mo	Tu	We	Th	Fr	Sa
1	2	3	4	5	6	7
8	9	10	11	12	13	14
15	16	17	18	19	20	21
22	23	24	25	26	27	28
29	30	31				

Irish Heath and Bog

Follow us on Twitter *@heath_and_bog*
for updates and links to our latest publications for writers

2021 Calendar For Writers

2021 Calendar For Writers Expanded Edition
(includes complete 30 Day Writing Notebook)

30 Day Writing Notebook

18 Month Calendar For Writers
(June 2021 through Dec 2022)

November 2021 30 Day Writing Notebook

Take 30 days and write your novel!
Get your first draft on paper in 30 days with this Notebook...

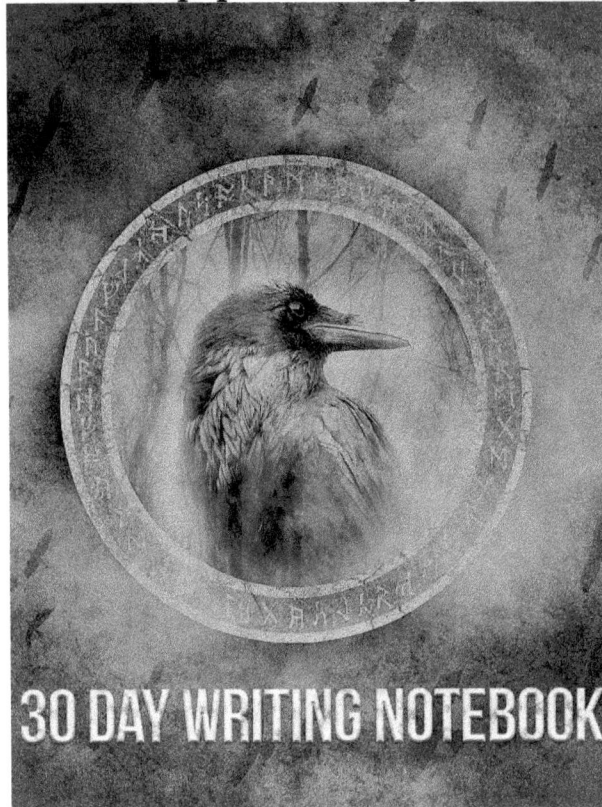

Available worldwide in 2021 at online booksellers

This is a basic Notebook designed especially for those who want to write their novels in 30-Day time periods. You can set your own pace: your writing days do not have to be consecutive, but you should aim to complete one day's work within 24 hours. Think of it as 'sectional' or 'segmented' writing: there is a beginning, middle and end to your daily output. For many writers, this can work to prevent 'writer's block', wherein you have an idea, but it doesn't necessarily 'fit' where you are at the moment in your draft, but you go ahead and write that segment; moving it later, in your second or third draft .. The point is to get it all down for editing later.

Divided into Week 1 through Week 4, each section contains 7 days with 8 pages (37 narrow lines to a page) to write on for each day. The 29th and 30th days follow Week 4. Each page is designed with a 1-inch margin on the left, a Word Count box at the bottom, and extra white space for additional notes and/or color/sticky note highlights. A Planning Page is placed at the start of each week. Five additional pages for Notes are appended at the end.

250+pp, 8x10in large format, glossy paperback

www.ingramcontent.com/pod-product-compliance
Lightning Source LLC
Chambersburg PA
CBHW080249030426
42334CB00023BA/2756